I feel better
'Relaxing visualisations to feel better'

Renate van Nijen

A collection of colourful paintings with a specific theme, combined with visualisations that will help you to feel better and/or bring relief on your path to health.

Original title: 'Ik voel me beter'
Published by: DMI Books.nl   May 2014

Translation and proofreading: Mandy Shanks, Lauren Sebastian and Carol Smart

Published by: Palcho Publication in collaboration with Ferry Verhoeve/ DMI Books
Layout: DMI Books

Website: www.renatevannijen.com

Table of contents

Theme of the paintings

All paintings in this book are oil paintings by Renate van Nijen with a special theme.

'Take your wings and sail away to your horizon of happiness, love and health'

In each painting you can discover 'two sailing boats' which are a symbol for freedom; like wings that help you let go of, and fly away from, all that is not good for you. There is also a 'red moon' in every painting by Renate van Nijen. This is a symbol for the Goddess Isis and represents, among other things, female intuition and creation (motherhood), health, healing and love.

Foreword

Over twenty years ago, I first discovered what visualising actually means by participating in a visualisation course. As a child and young adult, visualisation (daydreaming) was mainly a way to escape reality, simply staring into the distance and fantasising about the things I love. However, when I grew up I realised that I could also use visualisations in a very specific way in order to feel better. Fascinated by stories of people who claim to have been cured from mild to serious or even terminal illness through meditations and focused visualisations, I decided to further study the subject. A dear friend, who very much benefited from meditation and visualisation during her recovery from cancer, subsequently suggested to me that I create a small book of my paintings and visualisations.

As an artist I have had many years of experience in painting mainly colourful women and also in creating mandalas. Mandalas are wonderful to use while meditating and, from experience, I know that visualising a situation during meditation has a profound effect on me. Hence the reason I have felt drawn to create this book; a series of visualisations combined with paintings of women with mandalas.

I hope this book will inspire you to meditate and practise visualisation and that it may help you to feel better and possibly ease your path towards health.

Renate van Nijen

Visualisation, mandalas and chakras

In our modern society we will all be faced at some point with stress and illness and it is then often very important to be able to completely wind down. The relaxing visualisations in this book can help you with this, which will make you feel better and thereby enhance your healing process.

What is a visualisation?
Visualisation literally means: the translation of a thought into an image. So, you focus your attention on a thought and then create the image in your head. You could even say that visualisation is a form of meditation. By letting your mind relax, you can release your imagination to form mental images, drawn from a palette of tastes, smells, touch and other senses that are outside of your normal physical experience of reality. An increasing number of clinical studies suggest that meditation can help stimulate the immune system, reduce stress, depression and pain, can lower blood pressure, enhance a peaceful sleep and can even help fight the aging of the body's cells.

Especially for this book Renate van Nijen made a series of paintings with beautiful, intense colours and lots of symbolism. Each image has a mandala incorporated and seven of the paintings relate to the seven main chakras. Every painting is linked to a visualisation.

What is a mandala?
Mandala means 'circle' in Sanskrit and is a powerful symbol which we can find in various different cultures. It is a symmetrical design in a circle and usually a composition of colours, symbols and patterns. It is assumed that each mandala has a specific energy. Mandalas are often used in psychoanalysis and in healthcare in general, to aid the healing process. Apart from the fact that mandalas are lovely to look at, which in

itself often has a relaxing effect on people, they can also be used as a centre of focus during meditation or simply whilst chilling out. The first seven images in this book refer to, and have incorporated, the seven main chakra mandalas. Each painting has been painted in the specific colour of the chakra in question.

What is a chakra?

A chakra is a spiral-shaped, rotating energy centre in the body. When energy can flow freely in your body, which is the case when your chakras are working well, you feel good and you will be in balance. A sign that a chakra is out of balance or blocked can be that a certain problem keeps showing up in your life or if you have a physical problem.

How can I use the visualisations in this book?

The visualisations can help you relax and thus help you to feel better. Before you do the visualisation it is a good idea to do a relaxation exercise. (See relaxation exercise.) You can read the relaxation exercise and the visualisation of your choice a number of times, then do it with your eyes closed; or you can ask someone you trust to read it to you. You can also allow yourself to feel inspired by the image and experience whatever comes into your mind. There is no wrong way to do it. The relaxation exercise and visualisations are also available as an audio book. See: www.dmibooks.nl.

Relaxation exercise

It is recommended that you do a short relaxation exercise before you start a visualisation.

Go to a comfortable place where you cannot be disturbed and where you feel safe. Turn off your mobile/telephone/computer. Sit down in a comfortable chair with your back straight and supported. Place your feet flat on the floor. Of course you can also sit down in a lotus position or another position of your choice if you prefer. Your hands rest on your lap or on your knees, palms facing up. You may like to light a few candles and/or some incense. This can help to create a relaxing atmosphere. If you cannot sit up for physical reasons you can of course do the exercise lying down, but if you do lie down you may fall asleep and sleeping, while therapeutic, is not the same as meditation/visualisation.

Take a slow, deep breathe to the count of five and then exhale again in five slow counts. Send your inhalation to your belly and feel it extend. Continue to concentrate on your breathing. If you cannot inhale and exhale in five counts than simply do it in your own rhythm, for example in three counts. It is important that you become aware of your breathing. Try to imagine that a beautiful, soft beam of white light falls over you from the sky above. You are entirely wrapped in this wonderful light. Now this healing light also enters your body via your crown. Imagine the light softening your skull and your brain. Feel how they relax. Focus your attention on your forehead and relax. Now focus on your eyes and feel how the light is relaxing your eye sockets. Relax your eyes; relax your cheeks, your mouth, relax... the inside of your mouth... relax. Your entire head is now filled with the healing, white light. You now guide the light to flow via your neck, your throat, your shoulders and relax... Your thoughts take the light further down into your body: from your upper arms, your elbows and your lower arms to your hands ... relax. See the light streaming via your chest and your upper back down to your lower back and your belly. Feel how all the organs and muscles relax. The light now moves down via your hips and thighs, your knees, your lower legs and calves to your feet. Your entire body is now full of light and you feel totally relaxed. Continue your breathing for a while. Now take one deep inhalation and a slow exhalation and start the visualisation of your choice.

Note:
You can of course use this relaxation exercise as often as you like, whenever you feel like it. If you practise this relaxation exercise regularly you will come to a point where you can bring yourself into a deep state of relaxation simply by visualising the white light wrapping around your body and entering it via your crown, filling you with this healing energy and by taking a few, very deep and slow belly breaths in and out.

Which visualisations can I best use?

This book may well have caught your attention because you have some sort of a problem in your life. This can be a health problem, physical and/or mental, or a problem manifested in daily life, e.g. financial or relational. The intention of this book is to make you feel better. When you feel better you will have more energy and you will be better able to deal with the inevitable challenges in your life.

Seven visualisations in this book concern specific parts of your body. Thereafter there are another three visualisations which are about your future, listening to your heart and taking care of yourself.

This is not a novel or short story book. This book is intended to work directly on a condition or situation you are suffering from. In particular the various chakra visualisations are slightly similar. This is so as to make it easier for you to complete the visualisations on your own through practise by experimenting with various problems and or complaints you might be experiencing.

On the page prior to each visualisation you will find some explanation about the related parts of your body, the meaning of the chakras or the visualisation, but also about the meaning of the colours.

Choose a visualisation that can help you with a challenge you are currently experiencing in your life.

Ten visualisations

The ten visualisations in this book are accompanied by images of paintings which incorporate a mandala. Some people like to focus on a mandala or on the colours of the image, then (as recommended) do a short relaxation exercise, followed by a visualisation.

It is commonly accepted that doing a visualisation or a certain meditation at least once a day for a period of thirty days will help your subconscious to bring about the changes that can positively influence your health and/or your situation. For this reason, it is highly recommended that you do the relaxation exercise, followed by a visualisation of your choice, at least once and, if you like, two or three times a day.

The first seven visualisations are chakra visualisations, related to specific parts of your body. Please understand that if your chakra is blocked and doesn't function well this doesn't mean that you will also show all the symptoms. However if you suffer from a complaint at a certain spot in your body, the relaxation exercise and the visualisation can help you to let go of fear and negative thoughts. This can promote your healing process and help you to feel better.

Find a quiet, comfortable place where you cannot be disturbed and where you feel safe. You can light a candle or some incense if you like. This is your special moment! Sit down in a comfortable chair, your back straight and supported and your feet flat on the ground, or sit down in a lotus position. Now first do a relaxation exercise followed by the visualisation.

Muladhara

Muladhara

This is your root chakra which is located at the bottom of your spine. The colour for this chakra is red, the colour of vitality, power and determination. This chakra is related to trust, security and survival.

The parts of the body connected to this chakra are your back, your feet, your legs, your hips and your spine. If this chakra is not working well it can, for example, manifest in you suffering from an eating disorder, fatigue or arthritis. It is also possible that you feel unsafe, have a negative self image and/or suffer from survival problems. (Issues with shelter, food, etc.).

Muladhara visualisation

Relax. Close your eyes. Focus your attention on your breathing. Inhale and exhale through your nose. Feel how the fresh air is cleansing your body and how possible dark thoughts leave your body via your warm exhalation. When your attention drifts off, which can easily happen, you simply bring it back to your breathing. Notice how a white beam of light comes down from the sky. It entirely embraces you. This is a protective light and you feel completely safe. Slowly inhale and exhale a few more times. Go inside yourself with your thoughts and visualise a beautiful, intensely red sphere of energy entering your body at your tailbone. This energy opens the chakra, both at the front and the back of your body. See that your root chakra is flowing again with a beautiful, turning movement, like a vortex. Keep your attention focused on this while you breathe in a relaxed manner. Breathe in … breathe out…. Now go with your thoughts to the location in your body where you have a problem. Imagine the pain or your problem as a dark ball or spot. Quietly observe this, without judgement. When thoughts enter your head, simply watch them and notice how they leave again. Visualise how a wonderful beam of soft turquoise light enters your body via your crown. This healing light slowly goes to the problem spot or the pain. Whilst turning and pulsating on the rhythm of your heartbeat, the softening light embraces the dark ball or spot. See how it slowly disappears, little bit by little, until it has completely disappeared. Take your time over this. Feel how the pain diminishes. Know that this healing light will continue to heal you throughout the day. Stay seated for as long as you like. Then take three deep breaths, open your eyes and smile.

Svadisthana

Svadisthana

This is your sacral chakra which is located about two fingers below your belly button. The colour for this chakra is orange, the colour of happiness, optimism and the will to succeed. This chakra is related to intimacy, vitality, self-confidence and relations of trust with others.

The parts of the body that belong to this chakra are the reproductive organs,, the lower part of your intestines, your kidneys and your bladder. When this chakra is not functioning well you can, for example, suffer from lower back problems, stiffness, kidney or bladder problems or sexual problems. Perhaps you find it difficult to express your emotions or have a tendency to take on the problems of others. Some people can experience an uninhibited sexuality.

Svadisthana visualisation

Close your eyes and relax. Take your attention to your breathing. Slowly breathe in and out through the nose. Realise that fresh air is cleansing all the cells in your body and in your blood and visualise how any dark thoughts leave your body, again via the warm air when you exhale. When you notice your attention drifts off simply bring it back to the breath. Continue focusing on your breathing for a while. You now notice a white blanket of light from the sky completely embracing you. This is a protective light. You are safe. Take another few slow breaths. Inhale ... and exhale ... You then take your thoughts inside. Visualise how a beautiful orange sphere of energy is entering your body, about two fingers below your belly button. This orange energy revitalises the chakra, opening it both on the front and the back of your body. Your sacral chakra is flowing again with a gentle, twirling movement, like a vortex. You keep your focus on this for a while. Continue your breathing in a relaxed manner, slowly breathing in and out. Now take your thoughts to the problem spot in your body or your pain and imagine this as a dark ball. Observe without judgement. Thoughts are allowed to come and go; this is fine. Simply look at it and notice how they leave your head again. Now imagine that a beautiful beam of shiny, soft turquoise light is entering your body via your crown. The light slowly descends to your problem spot in your body or your pain. You see how this pulsating, healing light completely covers the spot. Keep your focus on this turquoise light. You have all the time in the world. Now visualise how the healing light is erasing the dark spot, little by little, until it has completely disappeared. Feel that the pain is getting less intense. This healing light will continue to work all day long. Stay seated for a little while longer. Take three slow and deep breaths. Open your eyes and smile.

Manipura

Manipura

This is your solar plexus chakra. The manipura is located slightly below your midriff, and slightly above your navel. The colour for this chakra is yellow, a colour that is associated with knowledge and success, with courage and taking action. The solar plexus chakra is related to your will, your self-worth and self-confidence; but also with power and control.

The part of the body that belongs to this chakra is your digestive system (stomach, liver, and gallbladder) and your upper back and the top of your spine. When this chakra is not functioning well you can, for example, suffer from heartburn or other stomach or intestinal problems, or diabetes. Perhaps you feel tired and without energy. It is also possible that you are afraid to say 'no' and find it difficult to take decisions or that you are suffering from tiredness or apathy or want to keep everything under control.

Manipura visualisation

Relax your body and close your eyes. Focus your attention on your breathing. Slowly inhale and exhale and feel the flow of fresh air coming into your nose. Imagine how the oxygen cleanses your entire body and feel how possible negative thoughts leave your body with a slightly warm exhalation through your nose. It is possible that your mind drifts off but that is not a problem. Just focus your attention back on your breathing. A beautiful beam of white light now encases your entire body in a protective way. You feel completely safe. Slowly take a deep inhalation and exhale slowly. With your thoughts you visualise that a beautiful, yellow sphere of energy enters your body just below your midriff. This yellow energy will open your solar plexus chakra on the front and the back of your body; you see how this starts flowing again with a beautiful rotating movement. Keep your attention focused on this while you continue your relaxed breathing; breathe in ... breathe out. Then take your attention to the spot in your body where you experience pain or a problem and imagine this as a dark spot or ball. Observe this for a while, without judgement. The thoughts that enter your brain are allowed to be there, but don't engage in them. Just look at them and watch how they leave your brain again. Now visualise a beautiful beam of soft turquoise light entering your crown. Your thoughts guide this light along to the problem area. The light is pulsating on the rhythm of your heartbeat and encapsulates the dark spot or ball with its healing properties. Little by little you see how the area is disappearing. You can sense that the pain has diminished. This light will continue to heal throughout the day. Stay seated for a little while longer. Take three more conscious inhalations and exhalations. Now open your eyes and smile.

Anahata

Anahata

This is your heart chakra. The anahata is located in the middle of your chest. The colour for this chakra is green, a colour which is associated with fertility and welfare. The colour green also has a calming and comforting effect. The heart chakra is related to love and appreciation for yourself and others, to empathy, but also to forgiveness and to desire.

The parts of the body associated with this chakra are your heart, your lungs, your thymus, your blood circulation and your blood in general. When this chakra is not functioning well you can, for example, suffer from high blood pressure, asthma or heart or lung problems. It is also possible that you are experiencing guilt or have an inferiority complex or suffer from relationship problems.

Anahata visualisation

You have your eyes closed and are totally relaxed. Now focus your attention on your breathing and feel how fresh air flows into your nose. This air is now cleaning your entire body. On exhalation possible dark thoughts will leave your body. Feel this warm air leaving your nose. If your thoughts start wandering, which is totally normal, you simply bring your attention back to your breathing. A beautiful, white beam of light is now falling over you. It is a protective light. You are safe. Take a few deep breaths in and out and take your thoughts within. Visualise a mesmerising, intense green sphere of energy entering your body at the level of your heart. This energy allows the chakra to start flowing again, both on the front and the back of your body. See how your heart chakra is rotating like a vortex. Keep your attention focused on this for a while and continue breathing slowly; breathe in … breathe out … Now go with your thoughts to your pain or your problem and imagine them as a dark spot. Observe this without judging yourself or anyone else. Should negative thoughts come up? Simply watch it happening and notice them leaving your head again. Visualise how a turquoise beam of translucent, beautiful light enters your body via your crown. With your attention you guide this light to the problem area. See how this healing light is pulsating and rotating on the rhythm of your heart beat and totally embraces the problem area. Little by little the dark spot is disappearing. Take your time doing this, until the spot has completely disappeared. Your pain will feel less intense and perhaps it has entirely disappeared. This healing light will continue working for the rest of the day. Stay seated for a little while longer. Then take three deep, slow breaths, open your eyes and smile.

Vishuddi

Vishuddi

This is your throat chakra and is located on the spot of your Adam's apple. The colour of this chakra is blue, the colour of the soul, but also of healing and idealism. The throat chakra is associated with communication, your inner voice, telepathy, clear hearing and with creativity.

The parts of the body that belong to this chakra are your neck, your mouth, the respiratory system, but also your shoulders, arms and hands. When this chakra is not functioning well you can, for example, suffer from a cold, or aches in your neck or jaws or from a poorly functioning thyroid. In addition, it is possible that you find it difficult to express yourself. You keep your emotions to yourself and often criticise yourself.

Vishuddi visualisation

Take a few deep and slow breaths and relax. Close your eyes. Focus your attention on your breathing. Imagine how the fresh air entering your nose is cleansing your body and how possible negative thoughts leave your body whilst you sense the warm air of your exhalation. When your thoughts drift off, which is possible, you bring your attention back to your breathing. Now notice how a white beam of light from above embraces your body. This is a protective light and you feel completely safe. Take a few more slow breaths. Now take your thoughts within and visualise how a beautiful, blue sphere of energy enters your body via your throat. This blue energy opens your chakra, both on the front and the back of your body. This allows for your throat chakra to flow again with a beautiful, swirling movement, like a vortex. Keep your attention focused on this while you continue breathing slowly and calmly. Now you turn your thoughts to your pain or problem and imagine this as a dark area or spot. Observe this for a while, without haste, without judgement. When you feel emotions coming up just let them be. Accept them, but do not try to explain them or dwell on them. Watch your thoughts come and go as from a distance, without getting attached to them. Now a beautiful beam of shiny, turquoise, translucent light is entering your body via your crown. The light finds its way to the problem area. Rotating and pulsating on the rhythm of your heartbeat the light encapsulates the dark spot or area. See how this healing light erases the dark spot, becoming vaguer and vaguer, until it has completely disappeared. Your pain is feeling less intense, perhaps it has vanished. Know that this beautiful light will continue to heal you throughout the day. Stay seated for as long as you find pleasurable. Then take three more slow and deep breaths. Now open your eyes and smile.

Ajna

Ajna

This is your third eye chakra which is located on your forehead between your eyes. The colour for this chakra is indigo, a colour which is associated with meditation, wisdom, individuality and mastery, but also with security. This chakra is related to clairvoyance and being able to see auras and chakras, but also with intuition, fantasy and being dreamy.

The part of the body belonging to this chakra is your head and to be more precise, your eyes. When this chakra is not functioning well you can, for example, suffer from problems with your eyes, headache or from neurological problems. It is also possible that you have nightmares or show some confusing and/or dreamy behaviour.

Ajna visualisation

Relax. Close your eyes. Now go with your attention to your breathing. Slowly inhale via your nose; feel how the cool air is cleansing your body and how possible negative thoughts leave your body via your exhalation through the nose. Should your thoughts drift off, which is quite normal, then simply return your attention to your breathing. Now visualise that a protective, white beam of light from the sky is embracing you. Look at this and feel that the white light is protecting you. You feel completely safe. Take another deep and slow breath and exhale slowly. Then go within with your thoughts. Imagine a beautiful, deep indigo blue sphere of energy entering your forehead, between your eyes. This indigo energy will open the chakra, both on the front and the back of your head. Watch how your third eye is flowing again with a wonderful, rotating movement, like a vortex. Focus your attention on this for a while and continue breathing in a relaxed manner; slowly in and slowly out. Now take your thoughts to the pain area or your problem. Imagine this as a dark ball. Quietly observe this without judgement. If thoughts enter your head then only watch them and notice how they leave your head again. Keep your attention on the dark ball, accept that it exists in your body, without giving it a meaning or explanation. Now you visualise how a beautiful beam of almost translucent, turquoise light is entering your body via your crown and descending down to your pain or problem area. Whilst rotating and pulsating on the rhythm of your heartbeat, the healing light is covering and enveloping the dark ball. You watch how this is being erased little by little until it has completely disappeared. Take your time to do this. Feel whether you notice a difference in your pain, has it reduced? Maybe it feels different to normal. Don't judge it. Know that this healing light will continue its healing power throughout the day. Take three deep breaths, open your eyes and smile.

Sahasrara

Sahasrara

This is your crown chakra. Your sahasrara is located on the top of your head. The colour for this chakra is violet, a colour which is associated with mystic, intuition and spirituality. Violet is also linked to discernment. The crown chakra is associated with meditation, insight, consciousness and knowing but also with religion in general.

The parts of the body that belong to this chakra are the central nervous system and the cerebral cortex. When this chakra is not functioning well you can, for example, suffer from epilepsy, but also from estrangement, apathy, boredom or depression and/or learning difficulties.

Sahasrara visualisation

Close your eyes. Take a few slow and deep breaths and feel how you easily find yourself in a state of total relaxation. Focus your attention on your breathing. Inhale through the nose, exhale through the nose. Feel the fresh, cleansing air flowing in and, with the exhalation, how any negative thoughts leave your body. This is a slightly warm sensation. If your thoughts start living a life of their own, which is very normal, bring your attention back to your breathing. Notice that a white beam of light from the sky is covering you. The light is embracing you, protecting you. You feel totally safe. Take a few more slow breaths. Now take your thoughts within. Feel that you are totally relaxed. A beautiful, violet coloured sphere of energy is entering your body via your crown. Visualise how this wonderful energy unblocks your crown chakra and helps it to start flowing again with a rotating movement, just like a vortex. Keep your attention on this while you calmly continue your breathing. Slowly inhale ... slowly exhale ... slowly inhale. Now you take your thoughts to your problem or pain and imagine this as a dark ball or spot. Observe this without judgement or trying to give meaning to it. Should thoughts enter your mind then simply watch them and notice how they leave again. Now you can see how a beautiful, almost translucent beam of turquoise light enters your head via your crown. Feel and observe how the healing light encloses and heals the problem area, whilst pulsating and rotating on the rhythm of your heartbeat. Watch how the dark spot is getting smaller, until it completely disappears. Feel that your head is becoming calm and relaxed. This healing light will continue to work throughout the day. Stay seated for a little while longer. Take three more calm and deep breaths. Open your eyes and smile.

Heart's desire

Heart's desire

It is your heart's desire for you to be happy. Your heart knows all your answers. Your heart knows that love can heal and in your heart lives love for yourself and love for the other. The colour of love is pink. Pink is the colour of the truth, peace, care and friendliness, but also of passion, trust and self-respect and respect for others.

This visualisation is about getting in touch with your heart and can help you find answers to certain questions. It is recommended that you do this visualisation regularly. This can reinforce your intuition.

Heart's desire visualisation

You are in a space or spot where you cannot be disturbed. You have just done the relaxation exercise. You feel calm and peaceful. Your eyes are closed. Focus your attention on your breathing. Breathe in and out via your nose. Feel how fresh air is cleansing your body and how possible negative thoughts leave your body via the warm exhalation. If your thoughts wander off, which can easily happen, you calmly bring your attention back to your breathing. Visualise that you are sitting under a tree in a large meadow with fresh, green grass and full of pink flowers. You smell the grass and take in the scent of the flowers. You hear birds sing and the peaceful humming of the honey bees. A soft breeze touches the skin of your face and you feel completely calm and safe. Now you notice how a beautiful, loving pink light enters your body via your heart region. Slowly this peaceful pink energy spreads further throughout your body. See how the energy spreads further outside the body, into the world, sharing your love with everything and everyone. Now go within and take your thoughts to your heart. Ask yourself a personal question, for example: 'what can I do to take better care of myself?' or 'what can I do to feel safe?' or another personal question you seek an answer to. Now calmly listen whether an answer comes up in your mind. Take your time to do this. Perhaps you notice a specific feeling. That is good. In case it is a negative feeling, for example sadness or jealousy; don't judge this. Simply let it be. Accept the feeling and hug it with love. It is possible that you do not immediately get an answer, which is fine too. Be aware because it is possible that the answer comes from an unexpected source in the form of an article in a magazine or a coincidental encounter. Know that your heart has the best intentions for you. Dare to be honest. Stay seated and listen for as long as you like. Now you take three calm, deep breaths. Open your eyes and smile.

Inner Child friendship

Inner child friendship

The inner child friendship painting is a colourful painting in which two women reach out their hands to each other. The colour for the visualisation belonging to this painting is white. The colour white is associated with the light, to purity, innocence and harmony. White, in fact, has all the colours in it.

Are you a people pleaser and do you usually totally ignore yourself? Then this visualisation can help you to bring about balance and to take better care of yourself. When you look after yourself you also have more energy to share with others.

In this visualisation you imagine yourself as a small child. You can also do this visualisation with someone in mind with whom you have a problem. In that case you imagine that you are standing in front of this person and see him or her as a small child. This can help you let go of resentment or see things more in perspective. Possibly it can help you to truly forgive this person so that you yourself can continue with your life.

Inner child friendship visualisation

You are entirely relaxed and your eyes are closed. Listen to the rhythm of your breathing and feel the cool inhalation entering your nose and the warm exhalation leaving your nose again. Visualise that you are inhaling a fresh, healing light and exhale dark obstacles. Now imagine that you are sitting in the shade under a palm tree on a deserted beach. You hear the calm soughing of the sea and you feel safe. Now watch a beautiful light of compassion and forgiveness entering your body via your crown. Slowly the light spreads inside your body, from your head and neck to your shoulders, arms and hands. Then via your chest, upper back further down to your belly and lower back into your hips and legs flowing down to your feet. The light is now shining in every cell of your body. You watch how this light of compassion and forgiveness extends, outside your body, into your direct surroundings and further into the world. Now take your thoughts back into a memory from your childhood, to a moment where you felt lonely or alone. Of perhaps you felt ignored? Possibly another memory pops up; that is fine too. Look your inner child deeply into the eyes and smile. Then hug yourself and say: 'you are safe, you will always be safe'. Feel how your love releases the pain or fear in your inner child. Take your time. Now bring your thoughts back to your spot on the beach beneath the palm tree. Look yourself deep in the eyes, as if you are standing in front of a mirror, and say: 'I forgive you for everything which you did not understand and for everything that you perhaps could have done better.' Maybe you want to forgive yourself for a specific action or feeling. You can then, for example, say: 'forgive me that I sometimes disregard you, for not always loving you ...' Hug yourself and give yourself all the love you have inside you. Enjoy the feeling. Then take three calm breaths, open your eyes and smile.

Esperanza

Esperanza

Esperanza means 'hope' in Spanish. There is always hope if you hold on to this and trust that better times are on the horizon, then you can transform your future. The colour of this painting is purple/violet, a colour that represents spiritual strength and points to higher levels. With your mind you can overcome and transform negative feelings and thoughts in order to reinforce your trust in the future.

This is a good visualisation for when you are worried about the future or if you have a specific wish you would like to come true.

Esperanza visualisation

Do the relaxation exercise. You are now completely relaxed and calm. Your eyes are closed. Focus your attention on your breathing at your nose. Feel how the cool air is cleansing your body and how any negative thoughts leave your body via a warm exhalation. If your thoughts are drifting off, which is normal, simply bring your attention back to your breathing. Visualise that you are walking in a forest with beautiful large trees. It is wonderful, soft spring weather and the leaves on the trees are an intense light green. The sunlight creates enchanting, golden patterns on the earth beneath the trees. Suddenly you see a stream with sparkling spring water. You feel great and drink from the clear, cool water. You discover a path right next to the stream, meandering its way up the mountain. You realise that this is the path of your future and decide to follow it. You see and hear the stones move in the rapidly moving water. You follow the stream up. Having arrived on the top of the mountain you sit down on a beautiful, grey-orange rock. You feel the contact with the earth via the strong rock and know that you are supported. You admire the fantastic panorama. A wonderful beam of soft-purple, protective light from the sky is now embracing your body. You look at the obstacles you have left behind and smile. You feel gratitude for overcoming your problems and are completely peaceful and safe. Then you see a large, shiny white sheet strung between two large trees. You observe your future on this screen. You are healthy and have a job that fills you with passion. You are surrounded by people who love you. Make the scene as lively as possible. Take your time. Smell the scents; hear the sounds... enjoy yourself. You now only feel gratitude for everything and everyone in your life, now and in the future. This feeling of gratitude stays with you all day long. Enjoy the feeling a little while longer. Then take three deep breaths. Open your eyes and smile.

About Renate

International artist and writer Renate van Nijen, born in the Netherlands, has been living in Andalusia, in southern Spain, since 2004, where she continues, to this day, to realise her passion for writing and painting.

The images in this book are also for sale as prints or post cards. On Renate's website you will find more beautiful paintings and mandalas, many of which are for sale as prints or cards. You can order these products from Renate's web shop via her website:

www.renatevannijen.com

I feel better 108

Various eastern religions, such as Hinduism and Buddhism, consider the number 108 as a sacred number. Prayer beads usually consist of 108 beads.

If you like, you can say the following sentence, or a positive sentence of your choice, 108 times a day, during a period of at least thirty days.

Every day I feel better and stronger. I am healthy and happy.

Inspiration

Inspiration for this book, part of a series of seven visualisation books, came to me via many books and courses in the field of esoterism. Via the Oprah Winfrey show my world further opened up and I started reading books by, among others, Gary Zukav and Iyanla Vanzant. Years later DVD's of 'The Secret', 'What the 'bleep' do we know' and more recently 'The cure is U' didn't tell me anything new, but were a welcome reminder of what I now feel is the truth. I noticed a subtle change in myself and it became easier for me to deal with 'problems' in my life. I was able to let go of frustrations and let go of anger very rapidly. I continued to devour books and information from, for example Marianne Williamson, Neal Donald Walsh, Joe Vitale, Esther Hicks and Mike Dooley. Each book and every little bit of wisdom have brought me to where I am today. I follow my 'path' and I do what makes me happy, namely writing and painting. I will continue learning and making new discoveries and be reminded of things I already know. Over the last few years I was especially inspired by information that came to me via MindValley of Vishen Lakhiani and in particular the 'Silva Method' and the 'Six phase meditation' were very inspiring for the writing of this series of seven books. I am extremely grateful for all these inspiring teachers who have crossed my path. I now wish that this book will inspire you!

Disclaimer

The information you can read in the 'The art of feeling better' series is intended to help you relax and to let go of possible negative thoughts, which will then help you feel better.

We do not claim that visualisations can heal you and we urge you to seek professional help in case you suffer mental or physical problems. These books are only there to support you on your journey.

In the series mentioned above you can find a lot of information about the meaning of colours, chakras, mandalas and symbolism. It is possible that you find contradictory information online. This is not important for the use of the books from this series as they are mainly intended to inspire you and to help you to relax.

Soon available in this series:

I can forgive
I feel better with astrology
I can give and receive
I follow my path
I am grateful
I can meditate